# ENDORSEMENTS FOR THE JESUS MOMENTS SERIES

"Jesus is always far better and far more interesting than we think he is, and seeing how the Old Testament points to him is a great way to find out how. These wonderful books will help us see more and more of Jesus."
**SAM ALLBERRY**, Associate Pastor at Immanuel Church, Nashville;
Author of *Why Bother with Church?* and *James For You*

"When we teach children that the stories from the Old Testament culminate in Christ, they begin to understand that he is the center of the Bible's story. This series highlights Jesus, the hero of every Bible story, and encourages readers to keep him at the center of their stories too."
**HUNTER BELESS**, Founder and Host of the Journeywomen podcast;
Author of *Read It, See It, Say It, Sing It*

"I smiled from ear to ear. My daughters came alive when they caught on. Hidden in this engaging true story is another *even more exciting*. We flipped backward and forward, all the while learning the biblical story and freshly encountering Christ."
**DAVID MATHIS**, Senior Teacher and Executive Editor at desiringGod.org;
Pastor of Cities Church, Saint Paul; Author of *Rich Wounds*

"We want our kids to see that the Old Testament points to Christ. In her marvelous *Jesus Moments* series, Alison Mitchell helps children seek and find the Old Testament connections to Jesus in fun ways they'll be sure to remember!"
**DANIKA COOLEY**, Author of *Bible Investigators: Creation; Bible Road Trip*™
and *Help Your Kids Learn and Love the Bible*

"Alison Mitchell draws children into a rich, true way of reading the Old Testament. The books are fresh, lively, attractive, intriguing and thought-provoking. Warmly recommended."
**CHRISTOPHER ASH**, Author and Writer-in-Residence at Tyndale House, Cambridge

"This *Jesus Moments* series is a delight! The clear and plain teaching of God's word, coupled with the intriguing illustrations and cleverly hidden symbols, make these books a win-win!"
**MARY K. MOHLER,** President's wife at SBTS in Louisville, Kentucky; Founder and Director of Seminary Wives Institute; Author of *Growing in Gratitude*

"What a clever series! By using symbols that children must find and explore, these books draw out significant links between Old Testament characters and Jesus. Perfect for parents and teachers who want to help their children understand God's big story."
**BOB HARTMAN**, Author of *The Prisoners, the Earthquake, and the Midnight Song*
and YouVersion's *Bible App for Kids*

Jesus Moments: Jonah
© The Good Book Company 2025

Illustrated by Noah Warnes | Design & Art Direction by André Parker | All rights asserted

"The Good Book For Children" is an imprint of The Good Book Company Ltd
North America: thegoodbook.com UK: thegoodbook.co.uk Australia: thegoodbook.com.au
New Zealand: thegoodbook.co.nz India: thegoodbook.co.in

ISBN: 9781802542943 | JOB-008066 | Printed in India

# Jesus Moments
## Jonah
### Finding Jesus in the story of Jonah

Written by Alison Mitchell   Illustrated by Noah Warnes

Did you know that the oldest stories in the Bible are a bit like puzzles? If you look carefully, you can spot some

### "Jesus moments".

These are moments when someone or something in the story is a little bit like **Jesus**.

So this book is the exciting true story of how God used **Jonah** — and a big fish — to rescue people who needed to turn back to him. But what makes it even more exciting is that it's also about **Jesus**, the greatest Rescuer of all.

As you read about **Jonah**, keep a lookout for some hidden **anchors**. Each time you spot one, that's a clue that there's a **Jesus moment** to find as well.

So let's get started…

The wind **roared**. The rain **poured**. And waves as high as a house crashed over the deck of the ship.

The terrified sailors did everything they could. But they were still sinking. And where was their passenger? Why wasn't he helping?

While the ship tossed and turned, the captain went below deck to find him. Was he hurt? Was he seasick? No — their passenger, **Jonah**, was…

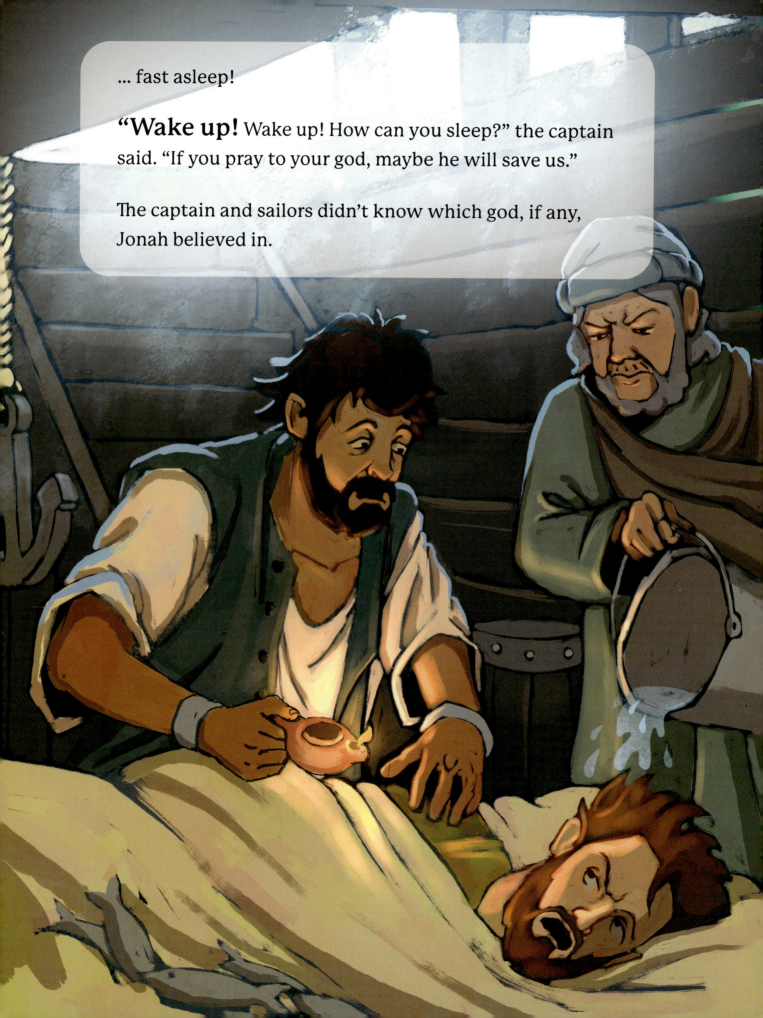

But then Jonah told them that he believed in the Lord God, the one who had made both the sea and the land. And that he was running away from God.

The sailors were terrified — this terrible storm had been sent by the God who **made** everything and **ruled** everything and who Jonah was running away from!

"How can we make the storm stop?" they asked Jonah.

"It is my fault that God has sent this storm," he said. "Throw me into the sea and it will stop."

The sailors tried to find another way… but they couldn't.

So, one… two… three… and overboard went Jonah.

Right away, the wind and rain **stopped**, and the waves grew **quiet**. Then the sailors knew it really must be the Lord God who had both sent the storm and stopped the storm.

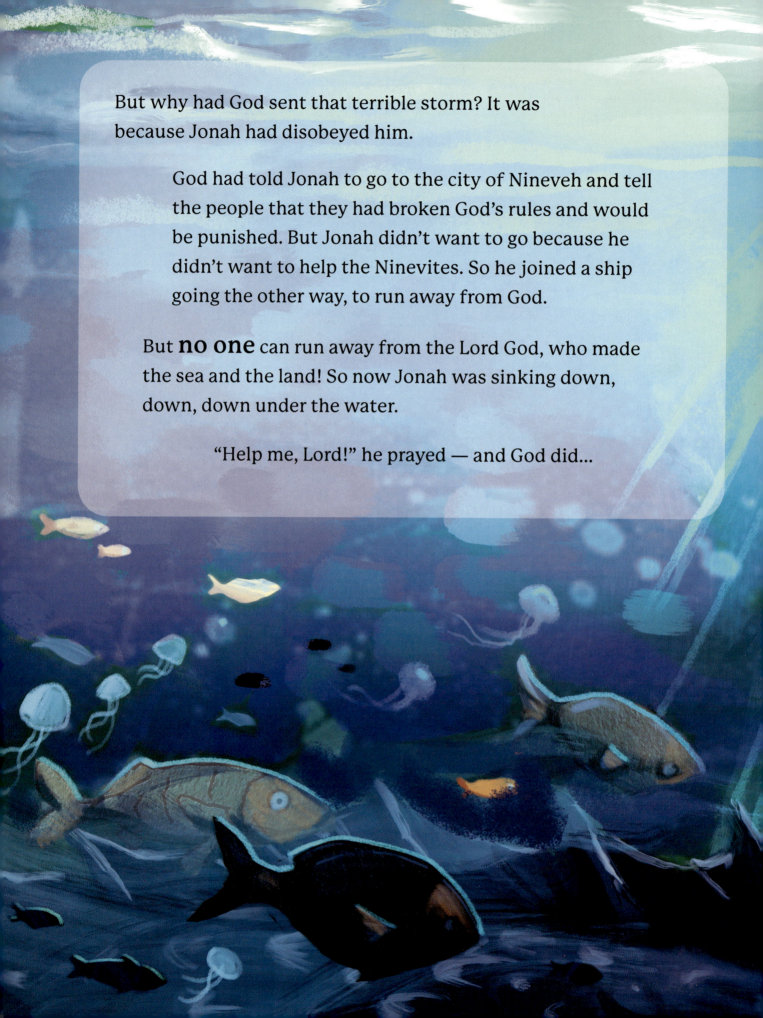

But why had God sent that terrible storm? It was because Jonah had disobeyed him.

God had told Jonah to go to the city of Nineveh and tell the people that they had broken God's rules and would be punished. But Jonah didn't want to go because he didn't want to help the Ninevites. So he joined a ship going the other way, to run away from God.

But **no one** can run away from the Lord God, who made the sea and the land! So now Jonah was sinking down, down, down under the water.

"Help me, Lord!" he prayed — and God did...

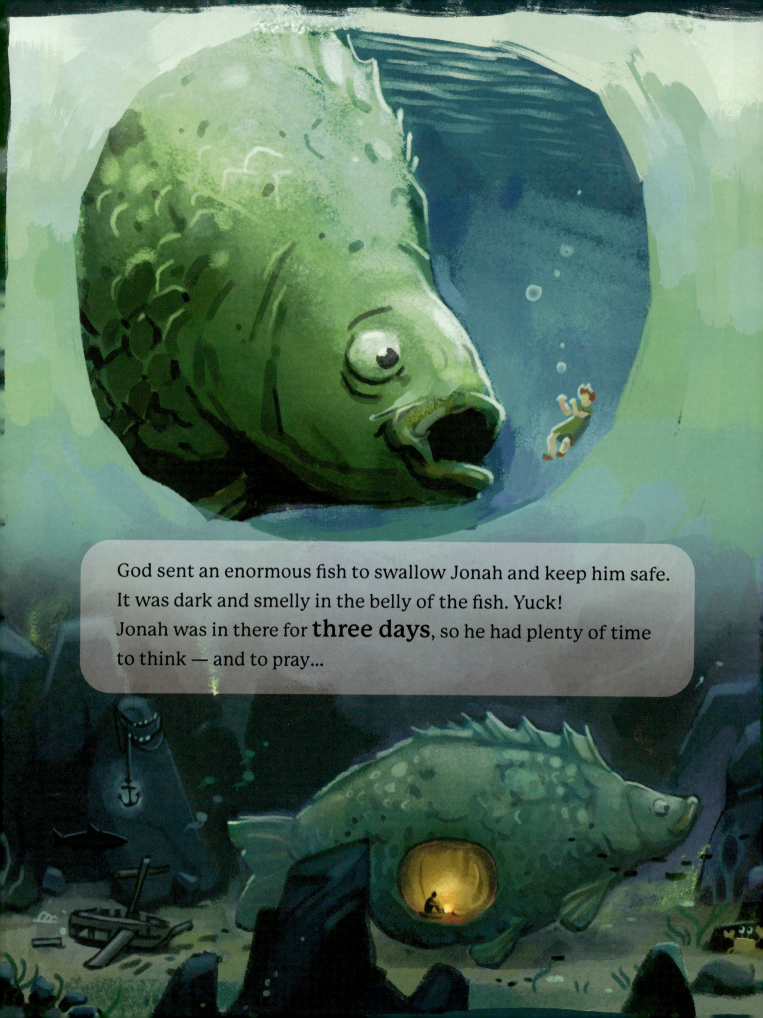

God sent an enormous fish to swallow Jonah and keep him safe. It was dark and smelly in the belly of the fish. Yuck! Jonah was in there for **three days**, so he had plenty of time to think — and to pray...

"When I called to you for help, Lord God, you answered me.
When I was sinking under the sea, you rescued me.
I will serve you and do what you said.
I will say, 'The Lord God loves to **rescue** and **forgive**'."

Then God told the giant fish to let Jonah go
— so it vomited him onto dry land! Yuck...

God told Jonah again to go to Nineveh, and this time Jonah obeyed.

"I have a message from the Lord God. He has seen how wicked you are. So God says, 'Forty days from now, I will destroy Nineveh'."

The people **believed** Jonah's message. They put on sackcloth to show how sorry they were. Then the king gave these orders to the whole city:

"Stop your wicked ways. Pray urgently to the Lord God. Maybe he will **forgive** us."

So everyone in Nineveh stopped eating and drinking, and they wore sackcloth. And when God saw that they had turned away from their wicked ways, he forgave them. The people were safe.

Everyone was **so happy** that God had forgiven the people. Everyone except...

... Jonah!

"I knew it!" he said angrily, "This is what I was trying to stop. You are the Lord God, who loves to rescue and forgive. Now you have forgiven the people of Nineveh — and I am **very angry** about it!"

"Are you right to be angry?" asked God, but Jonah didn't listen. He stomped off to a place from where he could see the whole city.

God made a leafy **plant** grow up high to give Jonah shade from the hot sun. Jonah was very happy about the plant.

But the next morning, God sent a hungry **worm** to eat the plant. Then God sent a hot wind, and the bright sun poured its heat onto Jonah's head. Jonah felt so hot and ill that he wished he was dead. And he was very angry that the plant had died.

"Are you right to be angry?" asked God. "You didn't make that plant grow, and yet you care about it."

"I did make every person in Nineveh, so of course I care about them."

And that was why God, who loves to rescue and forgive, **saved** everyone in Nineveh.

# ~~THE END~~

Stop! No. It isn't the end at all! It's time to spot some **Jesus moments.**

Look back at the pictures in the book. Did you spot the special **anchors?** They appear every time there is a Jesus moment in the story.

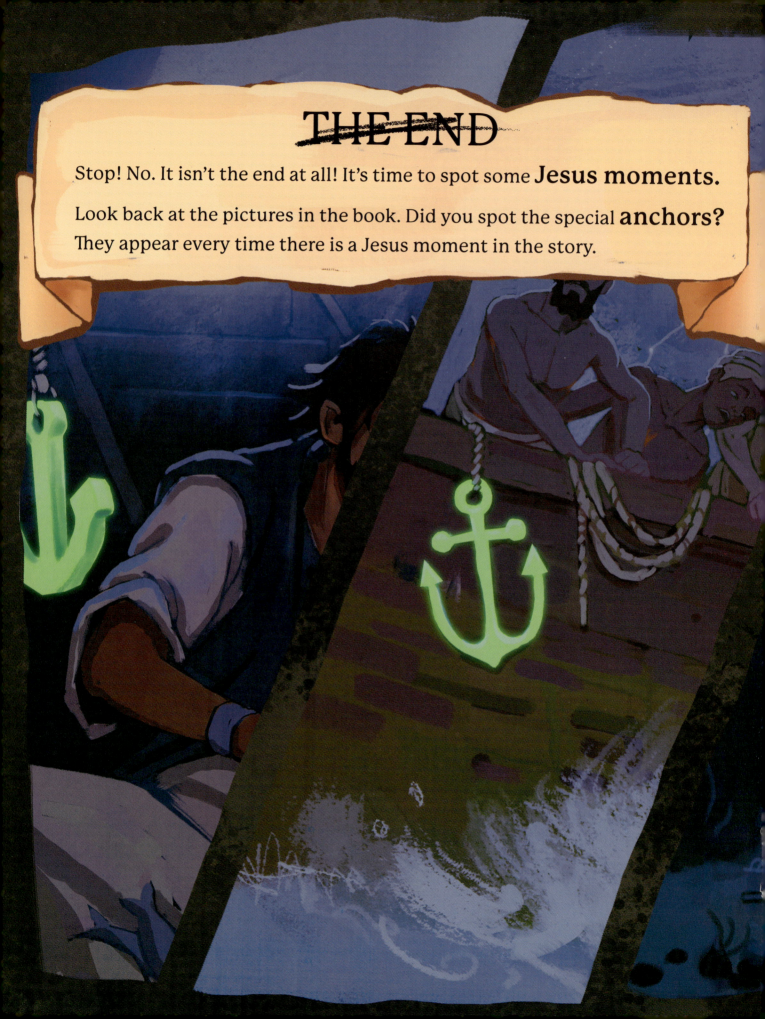

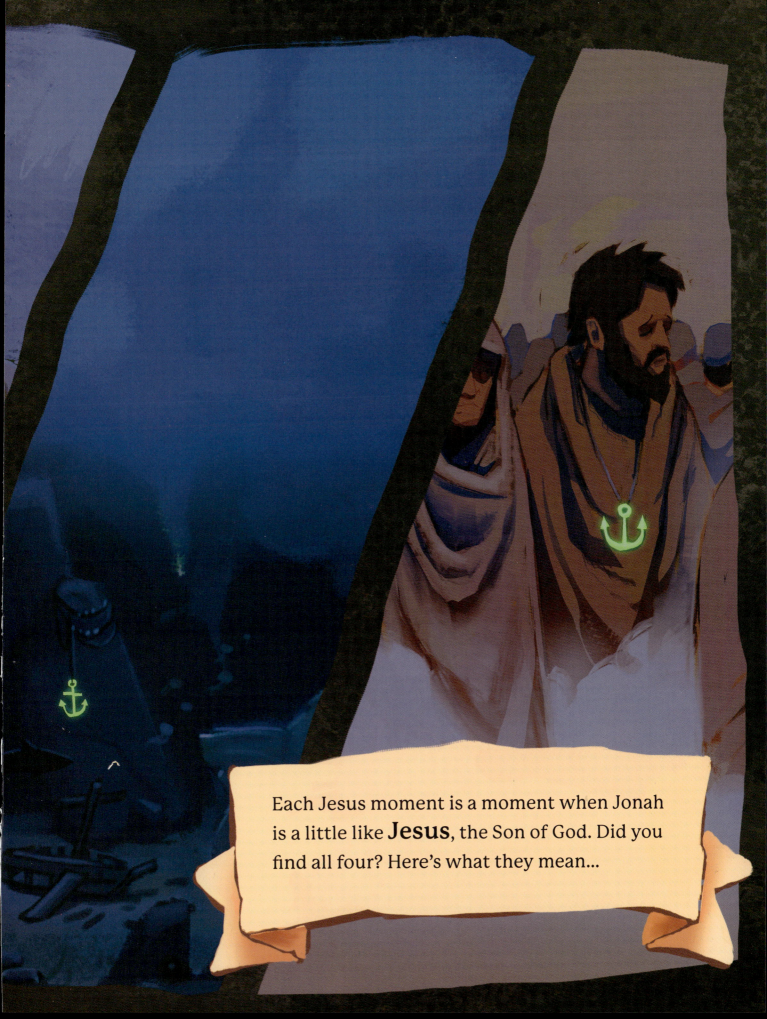

Each Jesus moment is a moment when Jonah is a little like **Jesus**, the Son of God. Did you find all four? Here's what they mean...

Jonah was asleep on a boat in a storm. The boat was nearly sinking. Only **God** could stop the storm and save the boat.

Jesus was once asleep on a boat in a huge storm too. The boat was nearly sinking. But when Jesus woke up, he stopped the storm and saved the boat, **himself!**

Jesus is far greater than Jonah. Jesus is God!

Jonah was thrown into the sea, facing death, because he **rejected** God and tried to run away from him.

Jesus was hung on a cross — and did die — but Jesus had **never** rejected God! Jesus died in our place because we are the ones who have rejected God.

Jonah spent **three days** in the smelly belly of the fish.
Then the Lord God told it to throw him out onto dry land.

After Jesus had been killed on a cross, he spent **three days** in a cold stone tomb. Then his Father God brought him back to life.

The people of Nineveh believed Jonah's message. They turned back to God and asked for his forgiveness. But this made Jonah **very angry** because he did not love the Ninevites or want them to be forgiven.

If anyone believes Jesus' message and turns back to God and asks him for forgiveness, they will be forgiven. And whenever someone does this, it makes Jesus **very happy** because he loves us and wants us to be forgiven.

Jesus himself spoke about "the sign of Jonah". He said, "The people of Nineveh turned away from their sins when Jonah preached to them. And now something more important than Jonah is here" (Matthew 12 v 41, NIrV).

Jesus is far greater than Jonah. He lived and died and rose again to show us that God loves to **rescue** and **forgive**.

# Why look for "Jesus moments"?

The oldest parts of the Bible were written hundreds or even thousands of years before Jesus was born, and yet they all point to him! And when we read the accounts of many Old Testament characters, we can see moments when they are a little bit like Jesus himself.

These "Jesus moments" help us to see Old Testament stories afresh and to understand more deeply who Jesus is and why he came.

In the Old Testament book of Jonah, we read about a very reluctant prophet. God told Jonah to be his messenger to the wicked city of Nineveh, but Jonah refused. Instead he tried to run away from God — something that no one can do! God used a storm and a huge fish to get Jonah back on course. At the end of the story, Jonah learns for himself how wonderful God's mercy is, which points forward to God's great love and mercy in sending his own Son, Jesus Christ, to die so that we can be forgiven (just as the people of Nineveh were).

It was always God's good plan to send his Son to live on Earth, to die for our sins and then to rise to life again. And God gave his people lots of clues about how this would happen.

The risen Jesus told his followers that the Old Testament Scriptures are about him: "And beginning with Moses and all the Prophets, he explained to them what was said in all the Scriptures concerning himself" (Luke 24 v 27). So when we read exciting Old Testament stories, we can look out for those same clues — those "Jesus moments" that point to the even more exciting story of Jesus himself.